CELEBRATING TIGERS

Celebrating Tigers

Walter the Educator

Silent King Books

SILENT KING BOOKS

SKB

Copyright © 2024 by Walter the Educator

All rights reserved. No part of this book may be reproduced in any manner whatsoever without written permission except in the case of brief quotations embodied in critical articles and reviews.

First Printing, 2024

Disclaimer
This book is a literary work; poems are not about specific persons, animals, locations, situations, and/or circumstances unless mentioned in a historical context. This book is for entertainment and informational purposes only. The author and publisher offer this information without warranties expressed or implied. No matter the grounds, neither the author nor the publisher will be accountable for any losses, injuries, or other damages caused by the reader's use of this book. The use of this book acknowledges an understanding and acceptance of this disclaimer.

dedicated to everyone who loves collecting tiger artifacts

TIGERS

Tiger, oh tiger, fierce and free,

Celebrating TIGERS

Bearer of stripes, a symphony,

Celebrating TIGERS

Your eyes alight with ancient fire,

Celebrating
TIGERS

In your kingdom, you never tire.

Celebrating
TIGERS

Through tangled vines and rivers wide,

Celebrating
TIGERS

You stride with purpose, un-denied,

Celebrating TIGERS

Each paw walking a thunderous beat,

Celebrating TIGERS

In the heart of your jungle seat.

Celebrating
TIGERS

In moonlit nights, you prowl and roam,

Celebrating TIGERS

Your presence felt in every home,

Celebrating
TIGERS

Yet in your gaze, there lies no malice,

Celebrating
TIGERS

Only the echo of a primal balance.

Celebrating
TIGERS

Your coat, a canvas of midnight's kiss,

Celebrating TIGERS

Each stripe a tale of untamed bliss,

Celebrating TIGERS

In the labyrinth of your design,

Celebrating TIGERS

Nature's artistry, pure and divine.

Celebrating TIGERS

With every breath, you speak the earth's tongue,

Celebrating
TIGERS

In the silence, your hymn is sung,

Celebrating TIGERS

Guardian of secrets, keeper of lore,

Celebrating
TIGERS

In your presence, we seek to explore.

Celebrating TIGERS

But alas, your realm faces a plight,

Celebrating
TIGERS

Man's greed casts a shadow, dims the light,

Celebrating TIGERS

Forests fall beneath the axe's swing,

Celebrating
TIGERS

And with them, fades the tiger king.

Celebrating TIGERS

Yet hope still flickers in amber eyes,

Celebrating
TIGERS

A beacon amid the world's cries,

Celebrating TIGERS

For in our hearts, the spirit thrives,

Celebrating
TIGERS

To ensure the tiger forever survives.

Celebrating TIGERS

So let us stand, hand in hand,

Celebrating TIGERS

Protectors of this sacred land,

Celebrating TIGERS

For in the tiger, we see our kin,

Celebrating
TIGERS

Bound by the same thread within.

Celebrating TIGERS

Let us weave a tapestry of unity,

Celebrating TIGERS

In the name of love and sanctity,

Celebrating TIGERS

And together, we'll write a new verse,

Celebrating TIGERS

Where the tiger's reign shall never disperse.

Celebrating TIGERS

For in the heart of every dreamer's plea,

Celebrating
TIGERS

Lies the promise of eternity,

Celebrating TIGERS

And in the tiger's majestic roar,

Celebrating TIGERS

We find the strength to restore.

Celebrating
TIGERS

So roam, oh tiger, roam once more,

Celebrating
TIGERS

Through forests rich, from shore to shore,

Celebrating
TIGERS

For in your stride, we find our might,

Celebrating TIGERS

Guided by your eternal light.

Celebrating
TIGERS

ABOUT THE CREATOR

Walter the Educator is one of the pseudonyms for Walter Anderson. Formally educated in Chemistry, Business, and Education, he is an educator, an author, a diverse entrepreneur, and he is the son of a disabled war veteran. "Walter the Educator" shares his time between educating and creating. He holds interests and owns several creative projects that entertain, enlighten, enhance, and educate, hoping to inspire and motivate you.

Follow, find new works, and stay up to date with Walter the Educator™ at WaltertheEducator.com

www.ingramcontent.com/pod-product-compliance
Lightning Source LLC
LaVergne TN
LVHW052005060526
838201LV00059B/3855